Standing on the Edge of the World

Lindsey Martin-Bowen

Standing on the Edge of the World

by
Lindsey Martin-Bowen

WOODLEY MEMORIAL PRESS
Washburn University
Topeka, Kansas

Library of Congress Cataloging in Publications Data
Martin-Bowen, Lindsey/ Standing on the Edge of the World
1. Poetry
2. Travel
Library of Congress Catalog Card Number

ISBN 0-939391-44-9

Woodley Memorial Press
Washburn University
Topeka, Kansas 66621
http://www.wuacc.edu/reference/woodley-press/index/html

Edited by Denise Low and Karen L. Barron

Cover design by Robert E. Haynes
Cover photo (back) by Carl Schiller Rhoden

For Carl, Aaron, and Ki,
and in memory of my father
Lawrence Richard (1927-2004)

Many thanks to Woodley Press editors Karen Barron and Denise Low for their expert suggestions. They've likely kept me out of trouble, an arduous task at best. Thanks also to my writing professors, David Ray, Dan Jaffe, James McKinley, and Robert E. Haynes, who have inspired and encouraged me these many years.

Acknowledgments—

"That Day in Williamsburg" published in *The Kansas City Star* (July 14, 2002). "Dancing with Aunt Virginia" from *River King Poetry Supplement* (Summer/Fall 2002). "March Ain't No Month for Poems" from *Best of Lip Service* (1994) and *Lip Service* (1990). "Alcatraz November" from *The Penn* (1994) and *The Kansas City Star* (October 22, 2000). "Late Autumn" from *The Same* (November 2003) and *Kansas City Voices* (November 2004).

"Snow Tracks" from *Lip Service* (1994) and *Number One* (1987). (This is part of a collection that won the grand prize in the 1986 Barbara Storck Creative Writing Contest).

"Periwinkle Park" from *Kansas City Voices* (November 2005). "Against the Current" from *Kansas City Voices* (November 2007). "Sledride" from *Encore* (Summer 1977, Vol. 11, No. 3). "She Could Speak of Mountain Sunshine" from *Lip Service* (1994) and *Summit County Magazine* (December 1979, Vol. 2, No. 3). "Working Toward the Last Line" from *Thorny Locust* (Vol. 10, 2/3 2002). "Kayaking" from *The Same* (July 2003). "Owed to No One in Particular" ("Elegy to No One in Particular") from *Boulder Community Free-School Catalog* (Spring 1975). "No Gingerbread" from *The Kansas City Star* (December 23, 2001). "Monkey" from *Review* (October 2000), *Any Key Review* (1999). "Hairdresser from Chile" from *River King Poetry Supplement* (Summer 2000). "The Landlady Says," *River King Poetry Supplement* (Summer 2000). "Truckdriver's Wife," *New Letters* (Spring 1987, Vol. 53, No. 3). "Bessie Smith's Adrift," *Lip Service* (1988) and *Number One* Magazine (1987). "Pruning Sweetpeas," *Shorelines* (1993) (Fourth place winner, *Shorelines* Creative Writing Contest, 1993). "Ellen the Tomato Lady's 84," *Shorelines* (1993). "To Etheridge Knight," *Kansas City Outloud*, an anthology (BkMk Press, 1975).

"Maestro in Central Park," *Number One* (1986). (This is part of a collection that won the grand prize in the 1987 Barbara Storck Creative Writing Contest.)

"Hanging Out in the Student Center" from *Lip Service* (1994). "Assisting Darvell" from *River King Poetry Supplement* (Summer 2001). "To Girl Taking Notes in the Victoria and Albert Museum" from *Coal City Review* (2007). "Another Place in this World a Woman Can Walk" from *SHOW + TELL*, an anthology

(Summer 2000). "First Night" from *Coal City Review* (2004). "At the Roman Baths" from *Number One* (1988). "Limousine Ride" from *Lip Service* (1989) and *Number One* Magazine (1988). "Tahiti" from *Thorny Locust*, Vol. 9, No. 3 (Fall 2001). "Other People's Memories" from *The Same* (August 2004). "What You Have" from *River King Poetry Supplement* (Summer 2001) and *The Kansas City Star* (November 4, 2001).

"Peter's Wife" from *Down Peaceful Paths* (Quill Books, 1991). (This poem was also on display at the Prairie Village City Hall and at Johnson County Cultural Arts-Entertainment Center. It will appear in a forthcoming creative writing text edited by Terry McFerrin Lowry.)

"Waiting for Glory in Winchell's" from *Black Bear Review* (Issue #16, Winter- Spring 1992-1993) and *Lip Service* (1991). "Statues" from *Review* (February 2002). "Mary at the Wedding in Cana" from *The Same* (Spring 2002). "The Day After" from *The Kansas City Star* (April 23, 2004). "It's Never Like the Movies" from *I-70 Review* (2004). "Standing on the Edge of the World" from *The Same* (December 2002).

Contents—

I Seasonscapes

II Another Place in this World a Woman Can Walk

III Two Brown Bears Dancing

IV Beyond the Vanishing Point

I

Seasonscapes

That Day in Williamsburg

Not far from the Atlantic, with its vicious waves,
we head south and swerve into a town (c.a. 1645)—
a Colony, a long footnote in history. There, red
Virginia brick surrounds a churchyard
so silent we hear the holly trees shivering.
It's cold, though frost
hasn't yet bit pumpkins or touched the squash.
The burning oak wafts from chimneys,
and we taste winter, acrid on our tongues.

In a stone bakery, we eat an old recipe—gingerbread.
We hold hands as if we were still lovers and wander
into a shop, antique blouses draping its dark walls.
Tourists step in front of us, weave
through us, push apart our fingers.
A Hispanic woman asks for a mob cap,
but the clerk doesn't understand what she wants.
I point it out, though I don't speak Spanish.
I hear her because I'm no longer myself.

When we head back to the city,
we know our season's winding down,
autumn rolling to its stop. Like the ocean,
it ebbs from this spot, where I imagine I float
out of the car, up and up. Shedding layers
of formalities that scale away like skin,
At first, I follow another breeze east.
Now I'm pebbles on a beach.
Then I become the sea.

March Ain't No Month for Poems
—to Alison Stone

Beats me—one day I ache to lie under an elm,
soak in a haze of smog on a concrete beach.
The next, I shiver, try to live without heat
in a one-room flat above a junkie who races
out at dawn to grab a tattered *Times*.

Each day, I watch him perk up or drag, shifting
like the mercury in a thermostat at my back window.
I'd swear I heard him scream last night about lice
inching up his quilt, scratching his armpits,
but can't remember for sure: I was blue then, too.

Seems my moods follow his trail like that,
and Alison, if *out-of-sight, out-of-mind*
translates to blind-and-crazy, I guess I'll
clamor through this night, jog on dew-slick
streets to score some kind of fix.

Dancing with Aunt Virginia

I picture a grove
where elderberries grow
and an old tire swing moans empty.
We go there before winds blow cold
and frost blots out windows.
She leads me to a spot by
rows of lilacs and pear trees
and teaches me to two-step in twilight.
We toss back our heads and stare
at a white gibbous moon glowing

like some dime on the pavement
I might walk tonight and grumble how
time's shortchanged her—evil Chronos,
the wizard who always wins. She, a dancer,
who taught me to waltz years ago,
can only move in her dreams,
where she unties her hair,
her black gypsy strands spinning,
and clicks the ghost of a castanet.

Alcatraz November

It wouldn't matter that I survive inside concrete.
But across the bay, lights glimmer, and a moon
lures me away from this island.
Seagulls dive and pluck orange rinds.
Some of them fly toward the sun.
Others loiter on reefs and fear an altitude
beyond stars that shimmer like palms.

I open one of my palms and trace a lifeline
smoother than any day I've stumbled through.
Then I squint at the west wind—
driving in a red and orange November.
I remember too much, and winter is in the wings:
it flutters steadily while the birds hammer gravel
and chisel food scraps from shore.

Dancers in Horseshoe Canyon
Wayne County, Utah

We focus our cameras, then snap the petroglyphs:
fifty narrow shamans without arms
under cliffs that canopy this silent ceremony.

A campfire smolders and turns these specters into dancers.
Like figures in strobe lights or silent films,
they sway across the huge gray slab and create ghost images.

The huge carved dancers stretch beyond the cliff overhead,
reach beyond the moon, beyond stars,
and whirl in the ghost dance of Wovoka—

who saw Jesus, scared settlers, drew
thunder from clear skies that roared into winds
to blow the Whiteman away—till the government outlawed it.

Tonight, one figure flickers before the tripod.
An Indian's knife stroke ties him
to this earth barren of tumbleweeds and sagebrush.

His black eyes follow us. We steady our shutters
And set our traps to snare his kinetic image
as his captures ours.

Late Autumn

with apologies to Theodore Roethke

Open your eyes, you say. Stop your dreaming.
But O—I take my waking slow.
Loathing the clock's incessant ticking,
ticking, ticking, clicking away, I pull
sheets over my head, dread the rushed drive
through slush and ice, the struggle
to stay this side of that tired yellow line.

Instead, I nod off, dream of elk
running beside a snowy shoulder.
Ice hangs from branches, glimmering now
like Andromeda, Cepheus,
and Cassiopeia. Light filters
through the aspen. We pull over
and race each other to a glen.

We smear snow over our mouths.
Then, leaning on trunks
a hundred years old, we pose,
switch places, click snapshots
of each other—despite
the shadows waiting, despite
our glimpse into where we'll go.

Above Timberline

Caribou Hill, Colorado

We bounce over a dirt road that winds into shadows
deep in a canyon where no one's stepped for years.
There, we stop, dig, and discover a femur.
I rub its chalky surface and imagine its past:
Maybe it held up a blond kid a hundred years ago
when he planted silver claims in Four-Mile Canyon.
His pocked face may have emulated yours today—
frowning and squinting into the sun, at the tundra,
and finally, at this bone I still hold.

Tossing back your hair, you become James Dean,
kicking the ruins, grinding boot heels on sacred ground.
Your words—"What junk!"—fall into my lap,
where I've placed my odd talisman.
I climb back into the Jeep, quiver and chug Almaden,
think about the flames that ate the timber town
in less than a day, here, on Caribou Hill, where now
narrow shadows spread and shacks split into dust.

Snow Tracks

The night is Alaska.

You trail southbound lights.
Fox-wrapped trapper ghosts
reflect in the white streets
as you walk in circles to
a stone mantel.

Your breath drifts backwards into your face.

Periwinkle Park

A ponderosa spreads along the edge
of Periwinkle Park. It's green—
green as Iraq TV scenes
shot at night in war zones.

We camp for the day, pretend
we're outdoorsmen—sit in vortex
under pines that smell
like bleached logpoles.

A fly circles me: its buzzing
interrupts the creek's high-pitched
refrain. The tiny beast
reminds me
how even in this place,
some annoyance
keeps me from letting go.

You unfold a topographic map,
search another route
into pines—far from the city
that squelched your dreams.
Clouds roil into battalions—
they cover the skies.
I think of Armageddon.

Mainly willows line the creek.
In the field, just one small aspen
intertwines with pines
that align like soldiers.

We share a can of kippers,
chase it with cheese,
pack into the truck,
wait for the rain.

Against the Current

This crazy blue river's so tough.
Wild as a woman caught in hot
flashes, lapses of memory, it whips
rapids into white caps, rages back
and forth, and winds through canyons,
switches back, cuts through an aspen grove
interspersed with pines.

We inhale scents of dying
fish, moldy leaves, then dip
our paddles into water, try to tame
this shrew, who, in a whim,
overturns canoes, sends men
to watery deaths
entombed by rock.

Like headstrong explorers
searching some pristine plot
of land, we grip till our knuckles
whiten, squint at eagles gliding
and plunging into waves. We push on,
yet regret entering
this insane race.

Sledride

Some wide-winged bird,
you rise over hills,
then down curves,
guided only by your torso.

Steering's rough
plowing your own path.
You're not quite sure
which way to turn—

whether to closely swerve pines
or fly down an open run
where rocks poke through ice.
So you swoop to the left,

nick an elm, shimmy on one runner,
then slide, not knowing
if snow's firmly packed, or
if there's an abyss under you.

It's hard to tell now
as you soar past barbed wire,
if you'll land in soft banks—
or fall from a cliff,
tailspinning.

Avalanche on Copper Mountain

to Chas—about our last run together

Snow hits hard
    against fogged
        glasses when
            we race each
        other down
    Copper slope.
        Knowing
            avalanches
                could split us
                    surges blood
                        through our chests.
                Then, your blond
            hair freezes,
                slaps your flesh.
                    Our cheeks char
                        with wind cuts,
                            knuckles pale
                    and fingers
                clench cold grips
                    as we glide
                faster than
                    love passing.
                Snow blots out
            trails. We spin
    apart in-
        to pines that
            edge our run.
        Steel clicks steel—
    we skid farther
        into
            ruts, where ice
                snaps our breath.

She Could Speak of Mountain Sunshine

of how white unfolds
like a canvas
over rock and black cliffs,
where a deer nibbles
a frozen stream.
She could list
every cliché that drove
her into the mountains
to escape the city days.

Instead, she watches a grizzly
scratch at her plastic window
as she digs out a .22 pistol
buried under her socks.

Tomorrow, she'll write of mountain sunshine,
smell pine and jasmine incense,
while her feet go numb.

Working Toward the Last Line

The night is Dresden.
Yellow and green explode in a black sky—
tracers flash, become veins
of webs hanging—
a cloud hovers like some lost ghost.
Branches crash into concrete.
Shell-shocked, we hear only sirens.
The whines keep us awake,
and this ignited night
burns to an ember,
leaving us without power.
We resent living
our ancestors' lives.

In the street, there's a line we can't cross.
This war against darkness
shows me how much
we're creatures of light.
But later, we walk, watch powermen
block off other streets,
where downed lines char asphalt.
A sliver of a moon
reflects off branches,
shimmering now—
this symmetry of ice.

August Heat

Brownstones doze in haze
that flattens this city.
Locusts hiss
like grease sizzling
in a pan or the traffic's
incessant hum over asphalt
so hot even drivers
in air-cooled cars roll on
as if simmering in crock pots.

It's 101—but not like July.
I know this will end.
Roses bloom
despite the heat. Their scent
urges me on.
I trudge uphill,
sweat grips my neck
like shrinkwrap.

It's always like this—
days I lug toward
some sweet breeze—
some vision shimmering
on this hot horizon.

Kayaking

A narrow thing, this plastic boat—
red stripes race down its sides.
And it's always a problem,
seeking balance,
trying to stay on-kilter.
We can't hop in feet first
but must wait till water settles
to slip into these kayaks.
With one misstep,
they'll overturn.
With one wrong stroke,
we'll run aground.

Paddling upstream's tough.
Dip left, dip right,
push against the current,
pull an oar left, then right.
Rolling on and on
through the waves,
we lose ourselves in the eddies,
we lose ourselves in the water,
we lose ourselves in sunlight
pooling around the shore.

We hit the breakers, then up and up,
in and out, back and forth,
laboring hard for breath,
like one who comes to the very end.
And then
we glide—
we glide—
o how we glide.

No Gingerbread

It's my first Christmas without them—
those ginger people my daughter and I baked.
Amid cinnamon smells, we'd twist
thick dough into shapes:
boys with raisin buttons,
girls with candied lips,
some with huge, deformed faces.
We built houses for the folk,
one year, a Swiss chalet.
Green frosting yards held cookie trees
and sugar baubles on branches.
I wired a light bulb inside it—gumdrop
windows became stained glass.
We turned off lamps, stared and dreamed
our sugarplum home was real.

She's miles away now in another city.
Baking seems futile.
I'll wander far from the oven,
through malls under tinseled eaves,
hang out in stores, pretend
I live inside Christmas cards.
I browse and read
James Tate to keep from sinking.
I'll drift over slick streets, focus
on red and gold lights,
buy a cheap tree,
stick a wreath on the door.

Cabs Don't Run in Viet Nam

Their engines choke on homemade gas.
I read this in the library, and now I stumble
home under rain that splats against yellow lines.
I spot a red cab with a black cabby.
He stares at me, slumps on an armrest, strokes
half-a-day's beard, and puffs a cigarette.
I don't hail him but stare south and picture
Asian cabs with Tiki lamps dangling from antennas.
Maybe now, between steel and glass, the cabbies picket,
tote signs about unfair business practices.
I'd thought that Viet Nam had been bombed
until nothing was left but bamboo shacks,
cathedral shards, shelled buildings, and a land
smoldering in dust and ruins.
This book showed me I was wrong about Viet Nam.
But it adds cabs don't run.

Everyone Connects Kansas with Oz

"... where you live is not crucial,
but how you *feel* about where you live is crucial ... "
—William Stafford, *Kansas Poems* (Introduction)

No Emerald City lies beyond the Flint Hills.
The bricks in Lindsborg and Cottonwood Falls
are rust-colored—not yellow. The thin blades of windmills
aren't like the Hollywood version of Dutch doll-
houses. And Kansas highways run from red clay
to asphalt black as obsidian.
No lions or tin men wait in the fields. Anyway,
Judy Garland hailed from Michigan.

What does it matter when wind twists along 40 Highway
as we fly by fields growing in thin topsoil?
We smell rain and scan the mauve and amber skies,
wait for tornadoes as we watch clouds roil,
and yearn for something eternal as the marble veins
around St. Fidelis's altar in the Cathedral of the Plains.

II

Another Place in this World a Woman Can Walk

Monkey

You say, "The monkey's coming."
I say, "No way," then spot him
bowing in a tiny red cap.

He dances like a sailor
drunk on grog
then spins around and begs.

A girl laughs, a boy yanks
his hair. Still the monkey pirouettes
and slaps a rail with his cup.

He scrambles toward us—the grinder
tugs his leash. Sorry-eyed, he retreats,
then leaps to his master's shoulders.

I clutch your hand. We embrace,
kiss deep and long. I feel his
tail grip my neck.

Hairdresser from Chile

Her vowels retain the Spanish lilt,
sweet caesuras, though she
came here thirty years ago,
bride to a tall, pale guy.
    Today, her black hair and eyes
reflect in my plastic drape.
She smiles, stares at fluorescents,
remembers her first night in this city.
    "My father-in-law said his Spanish:
 hot tamale, chili con carne.
I didn't understand—no such
words back in Chile."
Her mother-in-law barred her
from teaching her kids *espanol.*
But her son learned its soft sounds
after he saw a Mexican bleed to death
because no one knew his words.
    "I'm divorced now," she says, half-smiles,
loops my blonde strands over
her olive fingers, and snips their split ends.
"Left me for a young American blonde."
    The arc of her arm becomes
a black swan preening.

The landlady says

That girl was young,
honey-blonde, and
dressed to melt
a man to jelly.
She hung out with a guy
in a black Ford pickup.
They rolled out last night.
          All spring
she fed hummingbirds—
now I gotta keep
that red thing filled.
Look! There's one
dipping into a trumpet,

sucking in sap,
then it's gonna skit away
to some other garden.

Truckdriver's Wife

It's midnight.
Maybe he's doin' a run
to Shaky Town
where some lot lizard
checks his dip stick.

If he don't turn on his dog,
some bear'll nab him,
sure enough,
'fore he heads back to Windy
where chains nick asphalt,
and she shivers at a window.

Street Royal

A tall woman carries a
    cluster of jonquils
        wrapped in a *Wall Street Journal.*
Bareheaded, her tight curls
    form a headdress
        from some ancient tomb.
Her thighs
    rub each other
        and her jeans pinch,
but the arch of her lips,
    myrrh scents,
        and her long, smooth neck
reveal
    Egpytian
        aristocracy.
She stares at a thrift shop window,
    lifts her bouquet
        like a torch,
turns away from
    a rough wind.
        She moves on—
Cleopatra stepping
    over concrete, around
        a drunken Antony
slumped at
    the sidewalk's edge,
        saliva pooling at his lips.

Floating through Coffeyville on Pontoon Boats

Flood poem #3 (2007)

One of them wraps her hair in a bandana
to keep back the wind,
when three couples in their seventies tour
their neighborhoods again.
With waterlines above their windowsills,
white bungalows
surface for these odd gondolas.

I watch a river flow through streets cluttered now
with mildewed sofas and rotting crates.
Ahead an oil tanker seeps rainbows into the water,
and I wonder if Kansas is returning
to its prehistoric state.
Look—there—dipping into waves,
a pterodactyl waits.

Pruning Sweetpeas

At least on this dead branch, a few still green—
I'll steam them for my daughter Ki who loves these pods.
In my neighbor's yard, vines sprout, wind over our fence,
and strangle these sweet bushes.
She's too busy to deal with them.
Yesterday, she married her roommate, another woman.
They drove away in an eight-door Mercedes.
I'm not sure which one played the groom.
But I'm certain these brown and yellow twigs must go.
I yank twisting vines from sweetpea limbs,
tear away rotted stalks, and leave ripples of violet buds—
shaken, thinner, but pure.

Bessie Smith's

Adrift on whiskey
seas in a rowboat without oars.
Row me, Black Lady.

Assisting Darvell

He arches his back then swabs
her eyelids with topaz,
sea mist, and sand, colors
sending her to a beach
where she's Sandra Dee,
wading into sweet waves
foaming around her breasts.
      "Beautiful, Dahling,"
he says, then squints, sighs,
flicks a wrist and steps back.
      She blinks dove-like eyes,
focuses upon this Raphael
who clutches five brushes in one
hand, dabs another into
a chalky palette.
      An earring dangles
from his right ear, a stud punches
his left. He's from New York,
stationed now in Florida.
And for two days he must shiver
in our Midwest winds, glare at skies
muddy as the shades he avoids.
      I hand him a cotton swab,
chart his color scheme,
wonder why his thin wrist
draws these flesh portraits.

To Girl Taking Notes in the Victoria
and Albert Museum

London, England

You hunch over black boots with pointed toes,
scribble notes about women who stood rigid,
balanced bonnets above pedestals.

I, too, jot words about maroon drapes
that tremor inside dioramas. I note top hats,
Victorian lace, and a *cuirasse* ("a corset-like

bodice introduced in 1876"). That bodice
thrusts a mannequin's breasts with whalebone slats,
unlike the loose cape that wraps you in black.

You rest your forehead against a window.
Looking like a nun bent in prayer, you float through walls,
slip inside, and mingle with lives locked behind glass.

Assembly Worker in a Costume Jewelry Plant

Providence, Rhode Island

She flattens a gold sheet over a puncher,
then rakes back the black hair hitting her cheeks.
She tweezers broken glass into sockets.
It glimmers between her fingers
like the tiara she wore
in Aunt Nancy's dance class.
She pirouetted on rooftops,
jétèd to a tenement stereo's beat
and wore rhinestones
she pretended were sapphires, rubies,
or something as rare.

Today, the foreman lugs in
another box of baubles.
"For you," he quips,
grinning as if he cared.

Ellen the Tomato Lady

Flood poem #1, Kansas City (1990)

My neighbor Ellen digs in the trash again.
With back hunched, she lugs a plastic bag, swings it
into a green wheelbarrow, and drops it
onto a chair she scavenged from wet boxes
left on a curb. She glances at me furtively,
maybe thinks I'll condemn her like her husband
who hated gardening. When he died, Ellen dug
up one side of the yard and planted tomatoes.
"Put 'em in durin' a 30-mile 'n hour
wind," she says and squints at sunlight. Her cheeks
tell of a girlhood on a farm 18 miles
outside St. Louis. She moved here in '49,
and she says she wants to die in this neighborhood
where we pick each other's trash, stomp down mud
paths, and dodge washes of acorns as we push
kids in strollers that shimmy on sidewalks.
"Saved everything I could," Ellen says. "Grew up
in the Depression when you didn't toss a thing."
She hands me a plastic food cover
It looks like an umbrella with no stem. "Take this."
I touch it and smile, then follow a cottontail
that scampers on asphalt and darts into brush.
I pray he stays away from Ellen's tomatoes—
She's due for harvest.

To Etheridge Knight

Black poet on the stage:
I'm afraid.
I see men violent:
caged so long
their nerves vibrate hate.
Your Mississippi ancestry
taunts you at home
while I run
from Great-grandpa
who owned you
and still whispers—n
in my head.
I can't be you—
I touch your aching words,
but you won't call me sister—
Your brothers hate me.
I close my eyes,
blot out tumors of fear.

Black man on the stage:
I know plight,
I still run.
It ain't much better on the winning side.

Ellen the Tomato Lady Digs in Her Yard

Flood poem #2, Kansas City (1990)

Today, Ellen hoes her garden.
Her body curls over the earth—
as if she's some duenna guarding it from rain
that's tormented this land for a week,
leaving smells of dead grass, squirrel carcasses,
and water lines above windowsills. Still, Ellen digs on,
red bandana restraining her white strands.
Its ends flicker in wind while she hobbles,
upturning earthworms that a nearby crow eyes.
I stand at her gate, smell honeysuckle,
note that her yard needs mowing,
and her white clapboard house is too big.
But it gives Ellen space to dream.

I wonder if she hallucinates about giant tomatoes
dangling on vines that spread to upstairs windows.
She could enter the state fair with a prize
from that plump plant—or break apart the fruit and bake
a tomato pie. Perhaps instead, she pictures a hired
gardener bent over weeds. Maybe he rides a mower
and grooms her yard till it's as clipped as the leaves
Ellen crackles between her thumbs, gnarled as rutabagas.
She stops, rests her chin on knuckles,
watches a crow peck open seeds,
and wing toward the sun.

Ellen the Tomato Lady's 84

She doesn't want to live to be a hundred,
she says. "Don't want to be a baby
that can't do my taxes."
She fiddles with her sunhat,
wrestles a bag of leaves, twigs, and mud
that smells of musk,
tugs it to the curb, then shifts
her cobalt glance to her garden.
"This year, just got 800 pounds." She scowls.
"Usually bring in a thousand."
She purses her lips and limps
to the yellow plants that reek of sewage.
They twist around three wood crosses,
and I picture ship masts pressing
toward the Persian Gulf. A crew waits there
for its captain to yell, "Pull the lanyard!"
But Ellen doesn't talk of them or Saddam Hussein.
She rubs a callous, complains
too much rain ruined her harvest.
I ask if she has more tomatoes to vend.
She shakes her head and smiles, bends over her plants.
A red arch edges her neck.

Shadowing William Stafford's "Yellow Cars"

Black cars glare at me. Their bumpers grow gray
in the shadows. They sour
my hopes, feed my disillusions,
and remind me how today's bleak
shrill—like a finger rubbing
glass—won't quit
reverberating in my head.

Unlike the blasé tan autos
or the blue ones that dart
in and out of traffic
running me into the curb,
those black cars
leave me breathless
at an intersection
I can't yet cross.

To Salvador Dali
—About your "The Sacrament of the Last Supper"

Your Jesus is blond,
A blue-eyed guy, like the German
kid Dad wanted me
to marry. Light circled
his neck, too. Dad was proud
of his German blood, although

he was part-Jewish. Some say
Hitler was Jewish, too.
But his disciples lugged
Howitzers and flew Condors
with bent crosses. His black
hair and mustache didn't

look Aryan, like your
Jesus who breaks bread that
bleeds into shadows while
His followers bend. They
almost touch chins and
squinted eyes to red-tinged cloth.

Maestro in Central Park

In tie and tails,
the fiddler taps a wingtip.
His ridged fingers tug
a bow across catgut
that rolls resin into chords, catching us
when we walk under apricot trees.
Leaves brush his lined face.
My shutter snaps
his grimace.

With ghettoblaster backup,
he hums "*In quelle tine morbide*,"
then drifts to the Met's pit
where he brings down the house.

Hanging Out in the Student Center
to Bob

Everyone here talks about Lorca.
I can't recall who he was or what he wrote.
Faceless names, clever quotes—
wasn't it Pope who spoke of wit?
All this lit swirls into the haze that lifts off the Nelson.

I look at the gallery and remember
we jaunted its lawn to catch Caravaggio's
John the Baptist wrapped in maroon sheets.
You liked his thighs. But he was too pretty for me—
like the gigolos along Troost,

Greek minstrels waiting for gigs.
You liked those pretty boys, too.
You taxied them in a limo to their hot spots
until you quit college. Now you work in Washington—
a senator's office—and I returned to graduate school.

Today, ivy on Swinney Gym turns rusty.
I wander upstairs, meander like Borges through labyrinths
that Lorca maybe dreamed about.
I move downstairs and step onto a patio
overlooking the County Club Plaza trimmed with Christmas
    bulbs.

I'm Ferlinghetti riding a Ferris wheel over a midwest Coney
    Island.
Mink-wrapped shoppers dart in and out under green and
    red.
There's no encore to this scene:
No one claps, whistles or laughs.
And carnival lights flicker on and on.

Another Place in this World a Woman Can Walk

to Janet Kaufman

Here is such a place, if you don't mind flies
that slip inside the bag with the Coppertone. Mostly
retired folk sit on sundecks, shuffle cards, and squint
at the lake. At five, a bass shimmers above the
water. He snags a fly, then plunges below, ignores
the four poles we strung with minnows, stink bait, and
     worms.
Yesterday, I forced my bruised legs up a gravel
road that leads to The Steins, the Ozarks' "Last Resort."

This trip is my last resort, a last attempt to
bring peace to a man who has little. Today, he
grumbles about sweating his time at a family
business. I know what words hit him each day.
"Dammit!" "Stupid!" I grew up with that family's words.
Here, no such words trickle over the lake:
It glistens like sunlight on car roofs. I rock with it,
smell dogwood, and spot a heron landing
on an island. I could walk here, too, stroll boldly after dark.
No words would cut me like a fisherman's blade.

III

Two Brown Bears Dancing

First Night

We can't sleep
although we've been up since dawn.
It isn't the locusts singing,
Traffic's low moan, alfalfa smells,
or even traces of the Confederate ghost
who watched from a corner
while we made love.

Your heart beats almost
in sync with mine,
our stomachs growl,
and I wonder
what hunger
keeps us awake.

Other People's Memories

All we have are dreams of shorelines
dried up for those of us marooned
in Kansas. Here, the sea ebbed,
leaving bits of limestone shells
long before the Wyandot and Lakota
stepped onto these cracked plains.

I shut my umbrella, close my eyes,
pretend this rain liberates me.
I envision a scene with October sunlight
reflecting off waves along Seattle's shore.
The lapping water lulls me away
from memories:
a mouth gaping in an eternal "O."

A couple walks along the wharf.
She looks toward the sea,
always the sea.
He stares at the planks below.

Hand's Dairy—Specialists in Cream
and Produce since 1870

Bath, England

Red letters rust and peel off a dairy sign over the Roman
     baths.
A Caesar grips a toga, knots its stone bulk in clenched fists.
I laugh at the juxtaposition—words wither and paint cracks
on an ad for sweet cream and apples next
to a statue. Moss seeps over his cape and shimmers
in the wind that whips around limestone and circles his neck.

His laurel decays, too. It flakes into a pool
where once other Caesars, guards and gladiators
soaked and wrestled in steamy duels.
They came to absorb a cure from the green water.
Today, a guide warns, "Don't breathe amoeba mists—you'll
     catch TB."
While she runs on, I picture a milk factory churning cream,

and a farm girl toting a tin pail. She looks like Tess
of the D'oubervilles. And I see her run to Caesar,
watch them meander through grasses. This mismatched
couple holds hands and braids bodies together.
I glance back at the dairy sign
then wade into wet rust. My soles slide into slime.

At the Roman Baths

Bath, England

Friend, I'm bored. While you meditate in the States,
I write of lichen-coated legions
lurking over amoeba water
as if those warriors could ward off T.B.

But I'd rather slide with you into a London taxi,
press my black hair against your chest,
wait with you in Gloucester Station,
and pretend we take the tube to Rome.

Cathedral of the Plains
(St. Fidelis Church)

Victoria, Kansas

Even if it isn't the Temple at Nîmes,
we race each other through quiet streets
to this tall, limestone church that reigns
over Victoria, a town the British named.
Inside, I feel chills and wonder if a spirit followed us.
I squint at windows to see if it filtered through green
and red glass, and listen for rustlings of the Holy Ghost.

Here, white marble guards the sanctuary.
It spreads out like angel wings, this marble from Italy.
But St. Fidelis never stepped inside this sacred place.
Killed when he claimed, "One Lord, one faith,"
he left the earth in 1622, centuries before this altar
was shipped, before Volga-German farmers agreed
to lift a cross here and name a church after this martyr.

St. Fidelis studied law and taught philosophy,
fought cases for the poor, and like me,
when put off by too much aggression
and greed, dropped the legal profession.
No saint, I come from German farmers in Mankato,
where the prairie roils from rust to green,
acres away from this Plains Cathedral.

And burdened with uncertainties,
I wonder if I'm a tsunami or a soaring melody.
Under stained glass reflecting in corners,
I move to candles and drop in quarters.
Then I light two stubs and drop to my knees.
I cross myself, inhale sweet perfume,
and watch you lift your camera to snap these scenes.

St. Patrick's Day in Trace's Bar
South Kansas City

The guy with the green hair fades
in and out, swivels around
the stage, and strains to your drumbeat.
He hums with your cadence
and winks at a blonde who taps
her nails in staccato on her glass
and runs her tongue around the rim.

I watch her eyes narrow
and know she'll no more pleasure
him than you will me tonight.
She'll croon to a pretty man,
press her lips against his ear.
This awkward fandangle
locks me in a strange refrain.

Still, I linger in Trace's Bar,
sing backup from where
I sit. I've followed you from gig
to gig, and I'm tired of green-
haired men and blondes who two-step,
tired of being reminded
I once sang on the stage with you.

Limousine Ride

We get it free—an hour
ride, in one sweet, slick, gray
'82 Lincoln. Tim
tips his hat and opens
the door to a leather
coach. Black glass shuts out sun.

We cruise to the Plaza
and the Liberty Memorial,
whose pillar shoots
to the moon. You ask me
if we'll indulge in secret acts.
I say we can't get caught.

But no one along
the Paseo sees us kiss
or your tongue tickle
my breast. Not even Tim
sees us slide on suede as
our cowhide bed heads home.

Tahiti

We both abandoned lives
we no longer believed in.
        You squeeze my hand.
I finger your calluses,
scars from that other life.
        You cast seaweed knots
across my breasts
and whisper, "I love you."
Sea foam glistens on our thighs.
We follow this inlet to an island
green with cedars and moss-covered homes.
        I see Tahiti in your eyes.
Brown children scuffle across
white sand and plunge into coves.
Gulls dip through palm-trees.
Only sweat separates us, and
the sun warms our backs.
        We wade in deeper.

Peeling a Lemon

Mandolins aren't real.
You say you'll teach me guitar.

I peel a lemon, break sections apart,
and press them against glass.
Acid leaks into cuts from guitar frets,
deeper slits than a mandolin gives.
Juice stings my fingertips.

Teach me the mandolin, I say again.

Captain's Wife

That's his clipper run aground,
and he's bent over a wheel,
face twisted aloft,
shoulders starboard.
A fortnight ago, we danced,
him drunk on grog or ale.
I pressed my lips against his chest,
cast honeysuckle knots across his head,
scooped his hair in my calloused hands.

Tonight, waves splash against those masts.
Gulls twitch, then dive to rocks below.
And I want to join them,
swim till the ocean swallows me,
and I drift up, saved.

Retaliation

If I swore "I love you"
with words cold as yesterday's meatloaf
stuck in an icebox with leftovers you hate,
you'd twist them up as if
you were a picnic wind,
shredding napkins,
grinding hotdogs,
leaving scraps.

Instead, I'll write a lilac-soaked letter,
stick it down your throat,
and watch you spit out
the sweet death of a wet oath.

My father buys a fedora

like Eliot Ness, his TV hero
who wraps up gangsters into tight bow-knots
to place at Hoover's feet.

He fingers the smooth felt,
eyes his purchase in a mirror,
flips up the left rim,
and winks at Mother.
She shakes her head.

I picture him, trigger cocked,
stomping through speak-easies
where swarthy men in holster
harnesses guzzle gin,
flick cigars, and slide stacks of chips
across green felt.
I wonder about his other buys.

Ironing Mother's Wedding Dress

It's neither white chiffon,
nor a debutante design
in magazines where white
sprays across each page.
It doesn't glimmer
like the moon
that illuminates
this dress on my board.
      She wore gray,
a flowing forties' style—
lace crocheted across the bodice.
She was Katharine Hepburn
dressed for dinner at eight.

The iron steams, spits
water onto rayon, dribbles
a pool that puckers the waist.
I smooth fifty years of creases,
then find stains in between folds—
liver spots
on hands growing old.

Waiting for the Wake-Up Call
Providence, Rhode Island

Morning comes, and still her phone lights don't flicker.
Like rubies, they drop dull light on an empty chair.
She opens her eyes, squints at blinds, the wicker
basket holding her boss's notes, and the TV that mirrors
smoke from factories outside where clotheslines edge a blue
      pool.
The screen re-ran movies all night, but now, its silver has
      cooled.

His voice seems to echo from halls where porters call to each
      other.
They wobble with overstuffed bags and hit doors and
      sometimes buzzers,
while waiters clamor with trays of hard rolls and butter.
She stares at the phone and reaches for her AT&T card on
      the dresser.
She wants her boss's Brooklyn accent to fill her with its
      rhythms.
But it's only six a.m. She knows his call won't come till seven.

Before she left, they shared margaritas in a joint off Times
      Square.
They embraced on a bench under Central Park elms.
He ran his tongue around her ear, raked his fingers through
      her hair.
"We're crazy, but I'll call tomorrow," he said and was gone.
She sighs, punches for room service, and waits once more for
      his word,
garbled with static, to tell her where to turn.

Still Waiting for the Wake-Up Call

She swerves a rented Honda through Providence,
breaking thumbnails on a leather wheel.
Her cell phone mocks her—its ruby lights don't blink.
Easing off the accelerator, she squints through the
      windshield
and crawls along without spotting a sign
to tell her which street's real.
Behind her, an Impala tailgates. Its driver sneers.
She rears up through the sunroof, shaking her head.
"I'm lost!" she shrieks, "I'm not from here!"

What You Have
to a husband with Alzheimer's

for Marge

A pilot you were, and oh—you kept me flying.
We were kids kissing so intensely.
We slept with your hand cupping
one of my breasts, mine on your cock.
You claimed you wanted to die first
than go on without me—
till you flew off, lost
like cargo missing the stop,
unwinding down the tarmac.

I weave words into red and yellow
to bring you in for a landing, but you soar
above clouds, out-of-range from my earthy voice.
Who says longing is more intense than having?
They don't know your touch.
Today, I squint toward the west,
wait to see you glide to my door.
Squeeze my hand when you drift in.
And I will steady yours.

Two Brown Bears Dancing on Ice

Moving in patterns like starlight on teacups,
they waltz under a full moon.
He nuzzles her—she whispers in his ear.
"A fantasy," you say. "They'd hibernate."
But maybe fall crawled in late that year.
Seventy-degree days warmed leaves
that clung to trees long after their season.
Squirrels smelled lilacs, frolicked in yards
and didn't gather acorns till November.
This confused those middle-aged bears
who conserve every motion.
They lost track of days, forgot to mark
the calendar times to tuck in.
              Or maybe an avalanche
thundered over their cave, woke them
from dreams of honey and spring.
They grumbled, poked out noses,
smelled the strangeness
of white capping life.
Awed, they trundled out,
measuring each step.
Then the moon expanded—
lured them onto the ice.
A dream you say? No—I see them:
They shiver and hug,
fall into a two-step.
And it seems in the shadows,
they kiss.

IV

Beyond the Vanishing Point

Peter's Wife

How could you abandon me for a man?
Each day, I sit and weave sackcloth
that pulls apart like the honeysuckle
vows you scribble on parchment.
You say you'll be back now that skies churn black.
But I know you won't live in Capernaum again.
You won't fish again. You won't get drunk again.
We'll no more share our strange sin,
this earthy love.

Waiting for Glory in Winchell's

The black guy behind the counter grins so big,
his teeth reflect the six a.m. sun.
Got up too late for Mass, so I bite into an apple
fritter. Father Darey says it's best not to
push religion anyway—just lure our bodies onto
the road to righteousness. Amen, amen.
So I think of all that's seen and unseen.

And Jesus, I want to tell that black man about you
'cause now his smile wavers as he wipes down
the counter, shifts crumbs, and shoves back a sleeve.
And I want to lead the toothless man at the next table
down the glory trail. He scratches his bald head
and squints at a *KC Star*'s fine print:
it burns when he drops ash from his Winston.

Yeah, I want to drag them both to glory.
But I don't spout a word about the buzz
in my pectorals or the goose bumps I get when I reflect
about you stepping back from death, every sore healed,
all parts intact. Instead, I squint at
sunlight and hum about this strange, mad gladness,
pray maybe they'll pick up on the tune.

Owed to No One in Particular
(or to anyone at all)

This is your poem.
You may spindle,
mutilate,
and/or
fold it.

It contains
(1) geodesic domes of lilacs
(2) interwoven with dovewings
and
(3) horseclouds with flaming nostrils
and twilight eyes.

It is
your poem.
Do with it
what you will.

Mary Magdalene Rebukes Peter

"No wonder the gospel of Mary Magdalene had been buried in a cave in the desert for centuries."
—Leslie Marmon Silko, *Gardens in the Dunes*.

You hate the way
we huddle together,
foreheads touching,
hands clasped,
sharing our secrets.

Your face grows pale
as the sky on a cloudy
October night, and your
hooded eyes follow us
everywhere.
They corner us in the market,
where we finger
pomegranates,
shop for fish,
duck behind canopies,
gather grain, and buy
sweet oil to pour
on his feet.

At our gatherings,
you boast of your loyalty
and call me a whore
who will destroy him.
But he knows your game:
when I wail at his grave, you will
deny you walked with him,
deny you slept with him,
deny you knew his name.

Some Words Are Cheap
to Bob Stewart

"Some words are cheap," you say. I scratch a scar
and wonder if they cost a nickel or a cent
or if that adage "dime a dozen" holds here.
If I had a nickel for every word
I've scribbled, I'd be richer than Dad if he earned
one each time he drove Swope Parkway. He wished
for that reward one night when we rode to Cousin
Allison's. She and I played with Barbies
and used the words, "Dream House," "Ken," and "Corvette
      Stingray."
Dad's shop was on Prospect, a street that speaks
of miners chipping quartz or panning gold. Those days,
I spent my quarters at NuWay's and bit
into patties that crumbled from their buns.
Then a quarter could almost buy a burger
or, at least, fries. Why now, I drop two smackers
for a Whopper and read HUD blew nine hundred
bucks on a hammer. But today, our colognes
smell richer, right? They must, 'cause yesterday,
a man offered me a hundred dollars to spend
fifteen minutes with him. I wonder why he
won't give that for my words. Still, Dad did all right.
Out of his seven, I'm the only one
without a six-digit income. So I amble west
over cracks to United Super and picture
boxes of words stacked on shelves. Like diamonds,
they glimmer under fluorescent lights that smell
like dust. I squint at those boxes and shimmy
out a giant size. In today's economy,
I can't afford gourmet packages, styled
for the upper echelon or professors who've earned

tenure. I spin through a turnstile, unravel
tissue, spill handfuls of words, shove them
into my mouth, and spit them at a knock-kneed kid
who presses his black nose against the glass and laughs.

The Madonna

It's cold here.
I shiver above flames
in tiny red and blue jars
while you plunk in quarters,
light candles, then genuflect.

My son stepped through fire.
It darted from the eyes of throngs
that had fanned him with palms
the week before. Blood trickled from his skull
when he lugged a cross to Golgotha.

Some mystics say saints smell of roses,
saccharin as a Jerusalem summer night.
Perhaps some smell like gardenias.
But I give off no sweet scent.
It's the candles' perfume that fills the nostrils
of seekers who fall prostrate.
Far from my fingers, they bend
too low to touch.

Annunciation

You don't understand—I can't be
an almost-mother, a woman waiting
for birth, when I can't remember
the heat of thighs over mine. Now,
I've waited two hours in this clinic,
smelled urine, heard sirens whine,
glass shatter. Then like some cynic,

you slip in, poke and probe me,
stand before me in your white coat.
The room's too bright—white
on white. And fluorescent lights
turn your sleeves into wings,
folding over a clipboard of messages.
You snap off your rubber gloves and scowl.

Even if I'm only 15, I'm not lying,
although I can't deny I feel my body
feeding life within, this overwhelming
burden from the answer, "Yes."
Still, I am the girl
who doesn't understand
what's happening.

Chasing the Vanishing Point

We head West, skimming desert sands.
They swirl, nick our windshield, make
us squint as if we were going blind.
Ahead, a caravan drifts
East with Jesus, slows, then stops.
You become James Caan, steering
our Charger past the nomads.

Once, I followed Jesus to
red-and-blue windows in an
Arlington cathedral. He
spoke to me in silent words
that fell like irradiated
glass into my lap. I scratched
them to see if they were real.

Tonight flares light our desert
trail. They flicker like dying
incense and the candles in that
cathedral. There, I lit a
candle for my son, myself,
and my lover I hadn't touched
or seen for a hundred years.

Tomorrow, we'll brush sand from
our teeth and shake sweat from hair
as we fight shifting tracks on
our road West. I glance back once.
Jesus frowns. His eyes become
candles that flame blue. He
stares at us and waves goodbye.

Sheol or Gehenna

"Hell is other people."

—Jean-Paul Sartre

1

"Close your eyes," Father Holder says.
"Picture someone who caused you pain.
Admit it. Wouldn't you like to see
the person condemned?"
    The ancient Jews didn't talk about hell,
he adds, until Egyptians enslaved them.
They spoke of Sheol, a dark, silent spot
where all souls go and battle without words
as if they were in some arena.
In Sheol, spirits don't recognize each other,
but wander through black streets,
where they bump against more lost entities.
    I look above Fr. Holder's head
to a gold Jesus, smell jasmine incense
from the altar. I think of you, my love,
and pray again you regain your faith.

2

The priest tells us Jews later talked
of Gehenna's lake of flames
and shrieks from tortured creatures,
visions some preachers rant about today.
I wonder if some of those teachers of fire and brimstone
suffered in tenements with rats and roaches.
I wonder if rats crawled over their eyes,
scratched their flesh, pierced their babies' thighs—
bit soft necks like the rosy one
in front of my pew. The girl tugs
her auburn hair.
     I pray once again and remember
a landlord kicking a family
into a stone street. You say there's no justice.
But I rely on faith when I see the children shiver,
watch hate flicker in their eyes.
Like them, I smell coal burning
on a hidden lake.

Statues

On days like this, white skies
and black clouds set me shivering in that netherland
where nothing seems real.
A pale woman leans her head against a Mercedes dash.
Her white hair and smooth cheeks
cut a silhouette against black.
And she becomes a statue.
      Her cold marble look
makes me picture the Parthenon, where I dance
with Phidias's creatures. We wander outside pillars,
rest under ferns in a canyon, and stare at skies as blue
and gold as a Parrish print. Their arms
glisten even in a setting sun.
      I pretend they are humans.
Even though they outlive us, their muscles never atrophy—
bodies never bead sweat. I think about
how Michelangelo freed their forms,
how their eyes have no pupils:
They stare into the future
without flinching
and show no regret.

Mary at the Wedding in Cana

He claims his hour hasn't come.
Still, I hand him an empty jug.
and command servants to obey him.
Shaking his head, he quivers
like an olive tree in Gesemane.
It's time, I reply but won't boast
the woman's the first to know
when winds change direction,
when a story begins to unfold.

Hot winds brush his skin, and myrrh
wafts among the guests.
He prays, lifts a stone water-pot,
then pours out wine that shimmers—
rubies trembling under
the swelling desert sun.
He offers me the chalice,
his eyes void, as if in a trance,
his cheeks ashen, his fingers dun.

Front Step Sacrament

You pour me wine
that tastes like almonds.
I press Baklava between your teeth.
We huddle like pilgrims
on the front stoop
and watch clouds roil
into rain.

Little Political Sense

Zebar says you have little political sense.
He grumbles with other Sanhedrin scribes
in the Temple. Its pillars tremble when you whirl in,
overturn tables, upset cages, and let loose doves—
they spread wings and flock to altars. You squint at them and
      your
heart breaks open. Its two halves become dove wings spread
out in a sacrifice. And you don't adhere
to politics when you heal a blind man on the Sabbath.
His hands quiver as his eyes fill with water.

I, too, have little political sense
when I watch the Humane University dismiss
a spinster librarian who served there fifteen years.
The supervisor drove her mad—harped at her
like a magpie pecking eggs in a dove's nest. She can't
remember which day is which. She blinks dovelike
eyes. "They're trying to fire me," she repeats, clutches
her walking papers. Her void voice spooks me. I squeeze
her fingers and later try to reason
with her supervisor. But my words rebound
from the speech she drew with Roman numerals.
"Not doing her job," she argues, her eyelids taut
as steel. Her teeth glow like iridescent glass.
I shake my head. "Not so," I try to say, but she's gone
on to Roman Numeral II. I nearly choke
on her Channel No. 5 and chew
my lower lip. Her numerals stand like the pillars
in the Sanhedrin Temple, where you once preached love
of God and man. They will not bend. So I check out
of the library and brush the dust from my sandals.
And you exit the Temple, lug wood beams on your back.

Communion Minister

"This is my blood."
—Jesus Christ

Some come to me, like the boy with scaled eyes
who limps toward the altar. He presses
fingers on this chalice and squeezes till his knuckles whiten.
Others look away and move only to the bread—
perhaps they don't like the wine's bitter taste.
Perhaps they fear becoming St. Sebastian,
who faced a firing squad of arrows
plunging into his chest,
and lived—
till Emperor Diocletian
ordered men to beat him.

Where I grew up, the parish served only the wafer.
I wondered why that priest left us thirsty
for wine to course through us,
throbbing and pulsing
into tributaries to Galilee.
There, we'd wind past olive trees,
switch back and drift into sand,
into a desert touching the sea.
Salty as blood,
it'd sting our tongues.

Today I swallow this watered-down wine,
and wonder if it's lost its meaning—
if it's become rain, pummeling this land.
I hear it hit the roof, run through gutters,
the wet tin crackling
like breaking glass.

I Dare not Elevate Myself to Sainthood

for Trish Reeves

Ki tells me my aura's white, a sliver of the moon.
Once a blue, yellow, and red rainbow,
it settled into this color of saints.
If I were a saint, I'd be like the astonishing
Christina, who flew from her coffin
to the church roof to get away
from the stench of human flesh.

She rose from Hell, she said, where she saw
many friends, then spotted more
in Purgatory. But she didn't mention
who she saw in Heaven.
Later, she flew to far away places,
scaled towers, trees, and boulders,
and crawled into ovens to elude human smells.

But I'm no saint, even if I battle an evil
wind rattling my windows and chase out demons
who spoil my cookies and cakes.
They say saints suffer physically.
And though I struggle with an allergy,
autumn's moldy leaves and fungus
don't enhance my purity. Oh no,

they make me cough and sneeze:
give me no inner strength.
Instead, I open a window, gawk
at a girl laughing in the street
below and hear couples
dancing at daybreak.
But I feel no inner glow.

I close my shutters to their joyful noise,
let any white haze around me
rise above this room
to another universe,
beyond the stars
glimmering like sapphires
in a white-gold setting.

The Day After

The darkness still holds.
Clouds hang low, touch the road
winding to the plaza,
where blood stains white clay.
I could not scrub
those stones clean
after they beat him.
They beat him there—my son,
till his body became a red mosaic,

black tears streaking his face.
They scourged him,
not for killing, not for theft,
but for his words—those words
that rang through the Temple.
They echoed through valleys,
rushed like water against a shore,
struck the dust, tumbled
across our dry land.

Today, I sit under an olive tree
beside the river,
watch waves lap the bank,
hear them moan a bleak song
among the stones.
The river sheds scales
as it passes my flesh, aching.
And its currents sing in a clear voice,
while mine cracks.

It's never like the movies—

for my father

this dying: no background chords
rising to a crescendo,
no *adagio* of strings.
You watch these ants, instead,
trickle across peonies.
They disappear. And you
can't keep your grip
on that granite wall of reason
but slip downstream
into some wild current
till you run aground.
There, you search
for the deserted place, a Holy Land,
where Elijah met God.
Even if you're hiking
the Appalachian Trail, up
Standing Indian Mountain,
you watch vultures circle
in and out of clouds festering
into some murky, yellow soup.
And when lightning hits,
Father Davis says Hail Marys—
and there, on the horizon,
you see Wovoka whirl
in his dance of ghosts.

The Soul of Kansas Might be a Scream

You hear it late at night when the moon
becomes a sliver in someone's dream,
and ripples in the lake settle
into streams lined with algae and bass.
It might come from John Brown's ghost
or the specter haunting the WPA castle at Coronado Heights.
It could be wails from Bob Elliot, who died in a wreck
on the red trail winding down from the peak.

Perhaps it's the lonely moan of a locomotive
over plains where fires break through nights.
Maybe it's the shriek from the red-tailed hawk circling
yuccas in the cemetery where the snow never stays,
or from the western ridge where coyotes cry
and geese wing through wide, blood-red skies.

On Coronado Heights
(at 100 Degrees Fahrenheit)

". . . cities of gold are dust."
—William Stafford, "Coronado Heights"

Here Coronado found true gold,
at least, according to William Stafford.
I stand in front of the red stone castle
and look at fields below—a patchwork
of rust, green, brown stretching centuries wide—
and remember the conqueror sought Cibola,
the reputed gold city on a hill
beyond the edge of his world.

But today we search for something else on this plateau.
Like some Pawnee scout, you follow the red dirt trail,
and I stay near the castle away from the lizards,
step around yuccas and clusters of milkweed,
and pick a sunflower that smells like clay dust.
A white spider crawls from the flower's center.
I shake this tiny guardian into the grass
and wonder if it was once sacred as a scarab.

Then, a flash glimmers on the ridge,
raining gold over everything—yuccas, flowers and rock.
Under the stardust, a warrior moves toward me,
his body shimmering with the heat lifting from the horizon.
At first, the gold reflecting off his skull
makes me believe he's a Spanish explorer.
But no—he's a Quivira wearing
the helmet of a conquistador.

The Last Full-Service Gas Station

They follow us forever west, these ghosts of cattle drives.
They overtake us, race us through haze eating
the horizon, where specters of longhorns
wander beyond the Flint Hills.
On and on we roll, like the sea that once flowed
over this range, leaving shells inside limestone.
Then, across from alfalfa fields, we find it:
a station still offering full-service—
windshield wiped, oil checked, free air.

The green and white building reminds me
of a drive-in, where a car hop might bring
fries and onion rings to our window.
Dust eddies across the pavement
and whirls like a meadowlark in thick wind.
A gray-haired man ambles out of the shop.
He squints, smiles, scratches a hip,
then flags us to an antique red pump.
A sunflower falls from between his lips.

Standing on the Edge of the World

I'm tired of working this town, sick of selling
my body to soldiers who call out "Sally,"
"Nancy," or "Beth" in nights so dark
the moon isn't even a finger wide.
Maude's Pleasure Palace gave me no pleasure.
But I waited twelve years. An overturned
lamp and a match helped it burn.
No one saw me dousing kerosene on
rafters, carpets, curtains, and sheets.
If that madam had let me go, I wouldn't have
done it. Still, firemen got them out, all
but the one dead already. And she was gone
before the first flame, before
I stepped into the lobby.

From this hill, I watch the dayfolk below.
Bored with the news, they wander in and out of market
stalls, haggle over chicken and tomatoes, chase
their children. One boy climbs over a basket, grabs
a cluster of grapes, pops one onto his tongue.
A woman smacks him, tugs his wrist,
shuffles him to a car idling.
He studies me as if he could read my void heart,
as if I haven't learned to wrap feelings
tightly inside its folds. I smile,
hope he can't see the can of kerosene
under my bag. I must bury it or take it along,
toss it in some canyon, where coyotes
will sniff it, then run off.

Maybe it's safe to step out of the shadows.
After all, it wasn't a house women will miss.
It matters just to searchers, like the one spending
the night when his wife gave birth.

Maybe men will stumble through alleys,
like ants who've lost their queen, or maybe they'll go home.
I don't know but stare across the valley, try to scout out a
        path.

Now the smoke's cleared, and I smell burnt oak
drifting to this dark patch where apple trees line up.
I wait in dead weeds. A soft wind
whips my skirt, cools my cheeks, and I ache
to ride morning's wings through fields.
When a door closes, they say, a window opens.
I close my eyes and pray they're right.

Lindsey Martin-Bowen

Born in Kansas and an intermittent resident there, Lindsey Martin-Bowen teaches prose and fiction writing, literature, and cultural studies at the University of Missouri-Kansas City. She has also taught at Johnson County Community College and Rockhurst University. She wrote for the *Johnson County Sun* Newspapers and *College Boulevard News* for nearly a decade. She served as Associate Editor for *Modern Jeweler* Magazine, then owned by Vance Publishing in Overland Park. For about 12 years, she served as the editor and wrote a column and features for *The National Paralegal Reporter*.

Her poetry and fiction have appeared in *New Letters, Lip Service, I-70 Review, Rockhurst Review, Bare Root Review, River King Poetry Supplement, Black Bear Review, Thorny Locust, Review, The Same, Kansas City Voices, KANSAS CITY OUTLOUD*: An Anthology of Kansas City Poets, *SHOW + TELL, Down Peaceful Paths* (anthologies), *Potpourri*, and other literary magazines. In 1992, Paladin Contemporaries published her novella, *Cicada Grove*, which won the 1987 grand prize in the Barbara Storck Creative Writing Contest. Its first chapter placed second in the fiction category. The previous year, her work won the grand prize and first place in fiction in the same contest.

She holds an M.A. in English with creative writing emphasis and a *Juris Doctor* degree from the UMKC Law School, where she worked on the law review from 1998-99. In 1997, the UMKC Law Review published her comment, *Words from a Teller of Tales: Can Storytelling Play a Role in Feminist Jurisprudence?* which included her short story, "Caroline's Story." (She's also a Missouri Bar member, but she makes more money publishing poetry and teaching.)

With poet Carl S. Rhoden, she helped organize Second Sunday Poetry Readings at the Borders Book Store in Overland Park, Kansas, from 1999-2001.

9 780939 391448